D1607557

JOBS IN THE
U.S. MARINE CORPS

SIYAVUSH SAIDIAN

ROSEN PUBLISHING

NEW YORK

Published in 2023 by The Rosen Publishing Group, Inc.
29 East 21st Street, New York, NY 10010

First Edition

Portions of this work were originally authored by Taylor Baldwin Kiland and R. Conrad Stein and published as *Careers in the U.S. Marine Corps*. All new material in this edition was authored by Siyavush Saidian.

Cataloging-in-Publication Data

Names: Saidian, Siyavush.
Title: Jobs in the U.S. Marine Corps / Siyavush Saidian.
Description: New York : Rosen Publishing, 2023. | Series: Exploring military careers | Includes glossary and index.
Identifiers: ISBN 9781499469981 (pbk.) | ISBN 9781499469998 (library bound) | ISBN 9781499470000 (ebook)
Subjects: LCSH: United States. Marine Corps--Juvenile literature. | United States. Marine Corps--Vocational guidance--Juvenile literature.
Classification: LCC VE23.S26 2023 | DDC 359.9'60973--dc23

Some of the images in this book illustrate individuals who are models. The depictions do not imply actual situations or events.

Manufactured in the United States of America

CPSIA Compliance Information: Batch #CSRYA23. For further information, contact Rosen Publishing, New York, New York, at 1-800-237-9932.

Find us on

CONTENTS

CHAPTER 1

THE TIP OF THE SPEAR

The U.S. Marine Corps (USMC) ranks among the world's most decorated and elite military branches. Marines are often considered the ideal fighters, capable of traveling by air or by sea to do battle under any conditions, anywhere in the world. The USMC has a rich and lengthy history of honorably serving the United States in some of its most challenging and important conflicts. Marines are proud soldiers, eager to support other service branches to get the mission done. There is an old USMC saying, dating back to the late 1800s, that still inspires confidence in today's servicemen and women: "The marines have landed and have the situation well in hand."

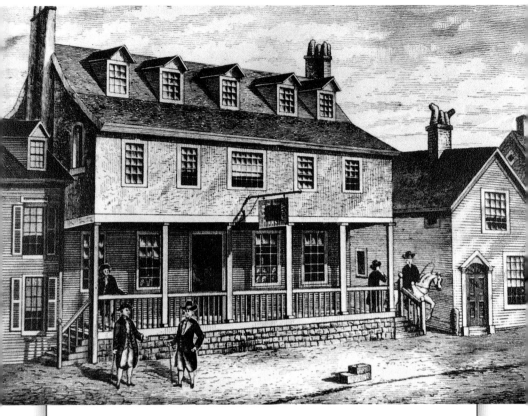

The modern USMC began in historic Philadelphia during the Revolutionary War.

BACK TO THE BEGINNING

In 1775, the United States was just beginning its war of independence against Great Britain. The Continental Congress—predecessor of today's Congress—established the Marine Corps on November 10. One month later, at the Tun Tavern in Philadelphia, Pennsylvania, the first official marine unit was recruited and formed. It was made up of 100 volunteer soldiers.

5

November 10 is now celebrated each year as the official Marine Corps birthday.

Using marines as sea-based soldiers was a tradition dating back to the British navy. In sea battles, British marine sharpshooters were asked to climb into the riggings of sailing ships to fire down at sailors on enemy vessels. The sharpshooters took special aim at enemy officers. British marines also disembarked from ships, rowed to enemy shores, and engaged in land warfare. A third duty of British marines was to act as a police force over regular sailors by breaking up potential mutinies. This unpleasant part of their job sometimes created resentment between marines and sailors, which can still be seen in the friendly competition between the USMC and the U.S. Navy today.

On March 3, 1776, the USS *Alfred* landed a small force of marines on New Providence Island in the Bahamas. At the time, war raged between the former colonies and their mother country, Great Britain. New Providence Island was a British stronghold. After 13 days of combat, the marines overwhelmed the British soldiers on the island while capturing 2 forts and seizing 88 enemy cannons. The ship-to-shore operation at New Providence Island was the first amphibious landing performed by the Marine Corps.

WHAT IS A "CORPS," ANYWAY?

Many people are surprised when they see "Marine Corps" spelled out for the first time, typically because it is pronounced like "Marine Core." Coming from French (and even earlier, from Latin), the modern use of the word "corps" refers to a group within the military—for example, the Marine Corps, which makes up its own armed service branch. Though soldiers who join the USMC are called "marines," it is often said that they serve "in the Corps."

SERVING THE YOUNG UNITED STATES

The United States gained independence from Great Britain in 1783. As an infant nation, it was weak, and foreign powers sought to take advantage of that vulnerability. One such foreign group was the Barbary Pirates, who called North Africa home. In 1803, President Thomas Jefferson sent navy vessels and several hundred marines to North Africa. Led by Lieutenant Presley N. O'Bannon, they were ordered to subdue the bands of pirates who were attacking American ships. First, the marines had to march 600 miles (965 km) over the scorching North African desert to reach a pirate-held fort in the state of Tripoli. There, O'Bannon and his men launched a bold attack in 1805. After a harsh battle, the marines defeated the pirates. For the first time ever, the American flag was seen flying above shores on the opposite side of the Atlantic Ocean.

Thomas Jefferson, the nation's third president, was among the first to use the marines to protect U.S. interests abroad.

However, things did not get easier for the young United States. A new conflict, called the War of 1812, broke out between Great Britain and the United States. In August 1814, Americans suffered a brutal embarrassment when a British army stormed their capital, Washington, D.C., and burned down many of the city's prominent buildings. Poorly trained and poorly equipped U.S. troops fled from battle before the polished, professional British soldiers marched to the capital. Only a small unit of sailors and marines put up real resistance against the British attack, though in the end they failed.

In the Mexican-American War (1846–1848), marines made landings on the Atlantic and Pacific coasts of Mexico. A marine unit was first to enter the gates of Mexico City. In September 1847, marines hoisted the American flag over the National Palace (later called the Halls of Montezuma) in the Mexican capital.

Throughout the 1850s, the major issue of slavery split the United States into opposing political and economic camps. In October 1859, an extreme antislavery activist named John Brown took over a government arsenal in Harpers Ferry, Virginia. Brown and his small band of followers urged slaves to rise up in rebellion and join him at the arsenal. Marines were the first troops to arrive on the scene of this uprising. A marine unit broke into the firehouse the group had turned into a fort and captured John Brown. The marines were led by Colonel Robert E. Lee of the U.S. Army, who would later become the famous commander of the Confederate forces in the Civil War (1861–1865).

Just as the conflict divided the United States as a whole, the Civil War divided the Marine Corps. About half of the men of the Corps resigned to fight with Confederate forces. Marines loyal to the Union served in sea battles at New Orleans, Louisiana, and at Mobile Bay, Alabama.

A HYMN OF BATTLE AND ACCOMPLISHMENT

Though the USMC is not quite as old as the U.S. Army, "The Marines' Hymn" is the oldest official song of any of the U.S. services. Legend says the earliest lyrics of the song were written in the 1840s by a marine on duty in the Mexican-American War, but this has never been proven. The melody came later, taken from a French opera called *Geneviéve de Brabant*. The first stanza of "The Marines' Hymn" reflects early marine engagements:

> *From the Halls of Montezuma*
> *To the shores of Tripoli;*
> *We will fight our country's battles*
> *In the air, on land, and sea;*
> *First to fight for right and freedom*
> *And to keep our honor clean;*
> *We are proud to claim the title*
> *Of United States Marine.*

BECOMING A WORLDWIDE FIGHTING FORCE

After the Civil War, government leaders considered dissolving the Marine Corps. Some believed that army troops could readily take over marine duties. Others argued that the country needed sea soldiers, working closely with the navy, to fight the "small wars" that often broke out in far-off ports. The government eventually decided to maintain the Marine Corps, although at minimum strength.

The "small wars" in the late 1800s and early 1900s kept the Corps fighting on fronts all over the globe. Marine units landed more than a dozen times on the coast of China to put down rebellions that potentially threatened American interests. Marines also performed similar missions in Panama, Nicaragua, and Haiti.

In the Spanish-American War (April to August 1898), marines were again the first to fight. Marines were the first Americans to land in Cuba and the first to storm the shores of the Philippines. Marines also occupied the former Spanish territories of Guam and Puerto Rico.

Just as in the early days of the United States, soldiers in the USMC faced serious dangers in early 1900s conflicts. They flushed deadly snipers from unseen positions and fought heated battles with rebels. Marines worked under the blazing sun while suffering from tropical diseases, including malaria. Still, some rose to the occasion beyond their duties.

In 1915, Sergeant Dan Daly fought in Haiti. While facing enemy fire, he pulled a submerged machine gun from a mountain stream. Daly's actions earned him the Medal of Honor, the highest award given to a U.S. service member. It was Daly's second such honor, the first coming from a 1900 battle in Peking, China. Dan Daly remains one of the few soldiers in U.S. history to receive multiple Medals of Honor, bringing pride to the Marine Corps.

The Medal of Honor is one of the country's most prestigious awards. More than 250 marines have been recipients.

ACTION IN WORLD WAR I

In 1914, World War I broke out across Europe. Many military leaders believed that the conflict would be short-lived. In the beginning, the war appealed to European patriotism. Soldiers marched out of villages while bands played and neighbors cheered. Before widespread fighting erupted, no one imagined the power and devastation that would be unleashed by new machine guns and enhanced artillery on countless battlefields. With these deadly new weapons, World War I became a conflict of ugly trench warfare. Huge armies fought each other from trenches, often separated by just a few hundred feet of scarred ground. In the miserable mud of those long ditches, the pride of European youth bled and died.

The United States entered World War I in April 1917 after Congress declared war on Germany. Upon arriving in Europe, marines and army troops encountered the same grim trenches where Europeans had fought for years. Like the Europeans, the Americans lived in the muddy ditches with rats and swarms of insects for company.

Though it is a marine specialty, the Corps did not employ amphibious warfare tactics in World War I. Instead, the marines were used as regular infantry. They often served under army field officers. In combat, all U.S. forces faced powerful artillery, poison gas, and deadly machine guns. In the summer of 1918, a fresh group of marines occupied a trench line just in time to meet a German offensive. The soldiers refused to flee in the face of that aggression, though European officers suggested retreat.

LOSSES AND VICTORIES

In June 1918, the Fourth Marine brigade repelled a German advance through a forest called Belleau Wood. During this historic battle, the young men were reminded of the war's brutality. Veteran German machine gunners rained deadly fire on the marines. In one day, more than 1,000 marines were killed or wounded. This single day at Belleau Wood marked greater losses than the total number of casualties the USMC had endured in its entire history. Still the marines triumphed, repelling the ongoing German assaults six times over the course of several weeks. German soldiers were so impressed with the fighting skills of these special American troops that they called them *Teufel Hunden*, German for "Devil Dogs."

World War I ended with an armistice signed on November 11, 1918, marking an end to a conflict that led to 20 million deaths worldwide. In addition to providing vital American support of allied Europeans, the marines achieved two great firsts during the war. On August 13, 1918, Opha May Johnson became the first female marine. During World War I, several hundred women served in the Corps, performing mainly secretarial duties. However, women were no longer allowed to serve in the marines after World War I. In July 1918, the 1st Marine Aviation

Air Force began operations in France. Marine pilots had trained in naval aviation schools earlier, but the World War I unit was the true beginning of marines working in aviation.

World War I became generally known as the Great War because of its global reach, huge casualty numbers, and destructive aftermath. Many even referred to it as "the war to end all wars" because people believed that humankind would never again make the mistake of creating such a devastating conflict. History had its own ideas on warfare, however, and just a few short decades later, World War II was on the horizon—and marines were ready to serve honorably once again in defense of their country.

Marines faced tough losses during World War I, but this conflict also marked the start of their record of excellence in combat.

CHAPTER 2

MID-CENTURY MARINE ACTION

In the years following World War I, the United States observed a general policy of neutrality when dealing with European powers. Even as Germany made aggressive advances in the late 1930s, Americans wanted little to do with another international battle. On December 7, 1941, however, Japan—a strong German ally—launched a surprise attack on a military base in Pearl Harbor, Hawaii. In response to more than 2,000 American deaths, President Franklin D. Roosevelt pushed for a declaration of war against Japan, officially pulling the United States into World War II. And it was against Japan, especially in the Pacific theater, that the USMC exhibited the elite fighting power for which it is still known today.

BRINGING BACK
AMPHIBIOUS WARFARE

With deep roots in amphibious warfare, the marines were more qualified, equipped, and experienced than any other armed service branch for fighting this type of conflict. Beginning in the 1920s, after marines saw little ship-to-shore action in World War I, General John Lejeune insisted the Corps return to its foundations and start using marines as soldiers of the sea. Just before World War II, General Holland Smith supervised training exercises in which large marine units practiced beach assaults. Two new landing craft were developed during the practice maneuvers. The Higgins boat was a flat-bottomed craft that held 20 to 30 assault troops. Men climbed from ships onto Higgins boats, which then took them to an enemy shore. Another landing craft, the amphibious tractor (called an amtrac), had tanklike treads and was able to climb up hostile beaches.

Many battles in the Pacific were fought as part of island campaigns. Island battles called upon marines' special skills in waging ship-to-shore warfare. American strategists viewed the Pacific islands as stepping stones or rungs of a ladder: Each island they could conquer would serve as an advanced base on the march to Japan. Airfields and supply dumps were built on the islands to mark the advance.

Furious combat took place on these Pacific islands. Japanese soldiers followed a code called bushido, or "way of the warrior." To them, dying in

Marines saw action in amphibious operations like never before thanks to advances in technology, such as the Higgins boat.

an honorable fight was acceptable and could even be glorious. Surrender, on the other hand, was an unthinkable disgrace. For more than three years, marines landed on the hostile shores of islands held by Japanese defenders who would follow bushido to their deaths. Nowhere to run with the sea at their backs, marines had no choice but to move forward against an enemy that had vowed to kill them or die in the attempt. Young men barely out of high school fought and died over small patches of land they had never heard of before—Guadalcanal, Tarawa, Kwajalein, Saipan, Tinian, Peleliu, Iwo Jima, Okinawa.

By 1944, nearly 500,000 men and women were serving in the Marine Corps. The American public praised the marines as elite infantry troops who could do the toughest jobs in the war. Hollywood pushed out movies celebrating marine heroism. For those fighting in the Pacific, however, there was no glamour in the war. They experienced island battlefields that claimed thousands of lives. In the jungles of the South Pacific, thousands of marines contracted malaria and other tropical diseases. Though their fighting provided a strong advantage to the United States and its allies, the horror of the island fighting took a toll on the marines.

GUADALCANAL: A "PARADISE"

In 1942, the Japanese were constructing an airstrip on the island of Guadalcanal. From the deck of a ship, this small island looked lush and green, ringed by a silvery white beach. It looked like a Pacific paradise to the 11,000 marines who were about to come ashore in August 1942. On the island, however, they discovered the hidden horrors of Guadalcanal: huge spiders, nightmarish land crabs, beetles as big as a man's thumb, and ferocious white ants whose bite stung like a needle.

As the marines were dealing with the natural dangers of Guadalcanal, the Japanese launched aggressive counterattacks by sea, land, and air to drive the marines off the island. Warships sailing off the beaches launched shell after shell at marine positions. Enemy planes dropped bombs. On the rainy night of September 12, thousands of Japanese soldiers charged the marines. The Americans fought back with machine guns, light artillery, rifles, bayonets, and even rocks and clubs. Marine lines held, but fighting continued across the island until the Japanese forces abandoned Guadalcanal in February 1943.

No other invasion symbolized the danger of World War II amphibious operations more than the marine operations in Tarawa. The tiny island of Betio, the main island of the Tarawa chain, is surrounded by a coral reef. Marines landed on the island in November 1943. Some of their landing craft were amtracs, which could crawl over the coral using their tanklike treads. But many landing boats were Higgins boats, however, which were not equipped with treads. Those on board the Higgins boats had to jump out and wade through a lagoon while enemy machine guns fired away at them. There was no path for escape and only one path forward.

The Battle of Tarawa lasted just over three full days, and it hit the USMC hard. Marine casualties totaled 1,027 killed and twice that many wounded. Months later, movie theaters in the United States showed films in which the American dead were shown floating in the Tarawa lagoon. It marked the first time in World War II that a movie showed large numbers of American dead. The movie showings were ordered by President Roosevelt, who wanted the public to better understand the sacrifice of their armed forces. Many people left theaters in tears.

A GUADALCANAL HERO

In a Guadalcanal battle in October 1943, Marine Sergeant John Basilone never stopped firing his machine gun to defend his fellow soldiers, even though he was surrounded by attacking Japanese forces. When that gun failed to fire, he held the enemy back with his pistol. Basilone was awarded the Medal of Honor for his actions. Following his award, he was sent back to the United States so he could march in parades and make appearances at other events promoting the war effort. However, Basilone did not feel good about being away from the fighting, so he returned to the Pacific. Sergeant Basilone was killed in 1945 when his marine unit attacked the island of Iwo Jima. A statue in his hometown of Raritan, New Jersey, honors his memory.

Sergeant Basilone's bravery in the Pacific theater made him a hometown hero.

CODING, OLD AND NEW

The Navajo Native American tribe played a major role in World War II. Throughout the Pacific theater, the Japanese tried to intercept American radio messages so they could anticipate their enemy's moves. Standard practice was to transmit messages in code, but the Japanese were skilled code-breakers. To counter Japanese intercepts, the marines used members of the Navajo tribe to relay orders by radio. Navajo is a complicated language spoken by only a few dozen people outside the tribe. The marines gathered about 400 enlisted men of Navajo descent and let them transmit messages. They were sometimes called "windtalkers," a nod to their Native American ancestors. The Navajos converted their ancient language to adapt to military terms: for example, *besh-lo* (ironfish) meant submarine and *chay-da-gahi* (tortoise) meant tank. This new form of "code" from Navajo words baffled the Japanese. No message intercepted could be understood by the enemy as long as it was broadcast by these Navajo "Code Talkers."

Navajo involvement in World War II gave the United States and its allies a valuable advantage when it came to protecting their communications.

A BATTLE AND A PICTURE

On February 19, 1945, a huge fleet of American warships surrounded the tiny treeless island of Iwo Jima. Battleships, cruisers, and destroyers opened fire with their big guns, and the island disappeared beneath the smoke of exploding shells. Early in the morning, dozens of landing craft, each filled with up to 20 marines, churned toward Iwo Jima. At the beach, ramps opened and the marines charged out. At first, Japanese defenders did not respond. Then, suddenly, artillery shells and gunfire struck the marines. The Americans desperately inched forward, crawling on their bellies like snakes. This landing marked just the beginning of the fighting on the island.

The furious battle for Iwo Jima raged day and night. On the morning of the fifth day, the marines fought their way up Mount Suribachi, an ancient volcano that dominated the island. At the peak of the mountain, the soldiers found a pipe they could use as a staff to raise an American flag. Men below cheered at the sight of their flag waving victoriously in the wind. Ships offshore blew their whistles in celebration. It was soon determined, however, the first flag was too small. A runner was sent to fetch a larger flag, and five marines and a navy medic raised the new banner. Journalist Joe Rosenthal photographed this second flag-raising, but at the time he had no idea that he had just captured the most famous image of World War II.

THE POWER OF IWO JIMA

By the time the marines engaged in heavy battle at Iwo Jima, the United States had been fighting in the war for more than three years. The public was getting weary of all the deaths and bad news coming out of Europe and the Pacific. Seeing the dramatic picture of marines raising the American flag on a bleak mountaintop thrilled the people and boosted their morale. The photo would become a part of American memory forever. On November 10, 1954, President Dwight D. Eisenhower dedicated the Marine Corps War Memorial in Washington, D.C. This massive statue features six marines raising the American flag on a 60-foot (18-m) pole in a larger-than-life recreation of Rosenthal's history-making photograph.

Marines working together to raise the American flag is one of the most enduring images of World War II.

The Battle of Iwo Jima dragged on for 36 days. Final victory came at a staggering cost in American blood: 26,000 casualties, including 6,800 dead. Survivors of the battle were left weak from horror and sheer exhaustion.

THE LAST ISLAND

Okinawa was the final rung on the ladder stretching across the Pacific toward Japan. On April 1, 1945, marines and army troops landed at Okinawa, all of them believing they were in for a terrible fight. To everyone's surprise, the Americans quickly gained control of the northern two-thirds of the island.

The real fighting took place in the south, and Okinawa proved to be the bloodiest battle of the Pacific war. Marines and army troops served side by side, trying to force the Japanese defenders out of their caves and bunkers. At sea, naval ships suffered repeated attacks from kamikazes, the dreaded Japanese suicide bombers.

No one on the island of Okinawa was aware of a top-secret operation called the Manhattan Project. The world's top scientists were developing the most powerful weapon ever created: an atomic bomb. At the time, Japan was a nation exhausted by the war and edging closer to defeat. Some American leaders did not want to use the new atomic bomb on such a weakened country. The inch-by-inch battles on Iwo Jima and Okinawa erased all doubts of the bomb's potential effectiveness. If U.S. forces had to invade the Japanese home islands, the casualty count for both Americans and Japanese was estimated at more than 1 million dead. To avoid such potential losses, a B-29 bomber dropped a single atomic bomb on Hiroshima, Japan, on August 6, 1945. Three days later, another such bomb fell on Nagasaki. On August 15, Japan surrendered to the United States and its allies. World War II, the most terrible conflict in world history, was over.

Marines are some of the country's most elite fighters and they are often tasked with some of the toughest jobs in war. Mainly due to heated battles in the Pacific, the total marine casualty count from World War II was more than 90,000 killed or wounded. Though the USMC provided less than 5 percent of the total American soldiers who fought in World War II, it suffered 10 percent of the country's casualties. This number was far higher than any previous marine losses. Even after such devastating losses, however, marines were prepared to serve again.

CHAPTER 3

AS TIMES CHANGE

Almost immediately following World War II, the United States was pushed into a conflict with the Soviet Union, its former ally. There were many contributing political factors that pit these nations against each other, but the most obvious was that Americans believed that the Soviet communist economic system was dangerous. This power struggle was called the Cold War because neither side openly engaged in fighting with the other. Instead, regional wars in Korea, Vietnam, and Afghanistan were the battlegrounds on which America fought with the Soviet Union. In these wars, the two sides generally supported the governments that supported their political ideals. For example, the Soviet Union aided communist-led North Korea while the United States supported capitalist South Korea. Throughout the Cold War, marines were on site to protect American interests.

A WAR IN KOREA

On the morning of June 25, 1950, artillery roared across the 38th Parallel, the dividing line between communist-ruled North Korea and South Korea. After the bombardment, Soviet-supplied T-34 tanks led thousands of North Korean infantry in an attack on their southern neighbors. The Korean War had begun.

American troops were rushed to South Korea to slow the communist advance. American-led forces were initially pushed backward on the Korean Peninsula, but they bravely defended a tiny corner called the Pusan Perimeter. On September 15, 1950, General Douglas MacArthur of the U.S. Army ordered soldiers and marines to land at the port city of Inchon, which was far behind the Pusan front. For marines, Inchon represented the last major ship-to-shore invasion they would make while under fire. Battling tricky tides as dangerous as the enemy, the marines established a beachhead at Inchon and marched inland.

The Inchon landings damaged the North Korean resistance. In late 1950, American forces drove deep inside North Korea. Then, late in December, bugles sounded over the North Korean hills. On cue, thousands of Chinese soldiers charged the Americans. The Chinese army had arrived to launch a new and ugly chapter in the Korean War.

This sudden attack left men of the 1st Marine Division trapped near the Chosin Reservoir.

Temperatures fell to 20 degrees below zero, and driving snow blinded the marines. In the face of brutal winds, the men began a 78-mile (126-km) walk to the port city of Hungnam. Only the wounded and dead rode in trucks.

The Korean War lasted for more than another two years as Americans and their United Nations (UN) allies fought communist troops in Korea. The American public was soon frustrated with the lack of progress overseas. Many simply ignored the events of the war. News of the Korean War stopped being front-page news. Some political leaders suggested that U.S. involvement in Korea was a "police action," not a war. The marines battling for the hills knew

This memorial in Washington, D.C., honors the marines and other American soldiers who fought in the hills and forests of Korea.

that this looked like war, smelled like war, and hurt like war.

It would take more than three years of fighting before an armistice was signed on July 27, 1953, officially ending the conflict. By that time, more than 33,000 Americans had died in the fighting. The agreement created the Korean Demilitarized Zone (DMZ) to separate North and South Korea.

In July 1995, President Bill Clinton dedicated the Korean War Veterans Memorial on the National Mall in Washington, D.C. Marching high off the ground are 19 larger-than-life infantrymen who move cautiously toward an American flag. Their faces bear the haunting expressions of men at war—confused, frightened, lonely. The monument stands as a powerful reminder of this costly war.

A NATION DIVIDED: VIETNAM

Not since the Civil War had Americans been so divided as they were over Vietnam. The Vietnam War began in the late 1950s when communist North Vietnam clashed with the armies of South Vietnam. Many believed this was a foreign civil war in which Americans should not intervene. U.S. troops were deployed first in small numbers, but their presence soon escalated to full-scale fighting.

Unsurprisingly, the marines were first to the fight. In March 1965, two battalions of marines—about 3,500 men—were sent to South Vietnam to protect an airbase at Da Nang. This was a dramatic change in U.S. policy. Previously, only advisers and other special troops had served in Vietnam. The marines were the first regular ground forces sent to the country. Those men of the Corps had no idea that their involvement marked the start of a war that would last seven bloody and frustrating years.

By 1968, one-quarter of the Corps' strength—about 85,000 soldiers—was serving in Vietnam. The marines fought major battles at Khe Sanh and in the Hai Lang Forest. The 25-day battle for the city of Hue remains a bitter chapter in marine history. Marines were hesitant to use artillery in Hue because it was crowded with civilians. Blasting the houses with artillery shells would create terrible civilian casualties. Instead, marines patrolled the city with rifles and fought the North Vietnamese and Vietcong street by street, house by house. More than 1,000 marines were killed or wounded in the ordeal at Hue.

Over the course of the war—from the first arrival of marines in 1965 to the final exit of U.S. troops in 1973—a total of 14,844 marines were killed in action, making up one-quarter of the 58,220 Americans who were killed in the war.

In 1982, the Vietnam Veterans Memorial was dedicated in Washington, D.C. The memorial consists of a black granite wall containing the names of the U.S. citizens killed in the conflict. It was designed to bind the emotional wounds the country suffered, and it is sometimes called the "wall of healing."

U.S. Marines paid a heavy toll during the Vietnam War, and this memorial shows the scale of their sacrifice.

FIGHTING IN THE MIDDLE EAST

In August 1990, Iraqi leader Saddam Hussein ordered an invasion of neighboring Kuwait, an oil-rich country. Iraqi troops occupied Kuwait despite the demands of the UN and other international authorities for them to withdraw. President George H. W. Bush sent American forces to other countries in the region. The forces of other nations joined them, and soon the Persian Gulf War began.

A full marine expeditionary force—made up of infantry supported by tanks, helicopters, and fighter planes—participated in the Gulf War. Minimum requirements for joining the Corps had risen in recent years, and the men and women who served in the Persian Gulf War reflected these higher standards. These were the brightest, best-educated marines ever sent to battle. Only half the Vietnam-era marines were high school graduates; nearly all of the Gulf War soldiers had their diplomas. Intense training prepared the marines for the desert warfare that awaited them.

Early in the war, the Iraqi air force was quickly neutralized, leaving the skies to the American-led forces. Marine fighter pilots worked closely with ground troops to eliminate Iraqi artillery, further increasing the security of the skies.

On February 27, 1991, fast-moving columns of marine tanks and armored troop carriers stormed Iraqi positions. At the time, many marine units were equipped with the aging M60 tank, which was generally seen as inferior to the M1 Abrams tank used by the army. Even so, marine tankers performed brilliantly at the Al-Burqan Oil Field during the largest tank battle of the Gulf War. In a heavy fog and amid smoke from dozens of oil fires, marine tanks destroyed dozens of enemy vehicles.

The ground operations of the Persian Gulf War lasted only two full days. In total, nearly 400 American servicemen and women (all branches) were killed. On the opposing side, estimates for the casualties suffered by the Iraqi army are up to 22,000 troops.

A NEW TYPE OF WAR

September 11, 2001, is a day burned into the memory of all Americans. On that day, airplanes that had been hijacked by extremists were slammed into the

World Trade Center towers and the Pentagon, and one crashed into a field in rural Pennsylvania. Almost 3,000 people were killed that day.

An underground group called al-Qaeda was responsible for organizing and executing this devastating act of terrorism. The group was led by a Saudi Arabian man named Osama bin Laden, who had his headquarters in Afghanistan.

Just days after the terrorist attacks, American special forces flew to Afghanistan and began the hunt for bin Laden. In late November, the first regular troops landed in the country, ready to fight. Those regulars were U.S. Marines.

The September 11 attacks, organized by Osama bin Laden, kicked off a lengthy conflict in the Middle East that saw extensive USMC involvement.

By December of that year, marines from the 26th Marine Expeditionary Unit (MEU) captured the Kandahar Airport and established one of the first coalition command centers in the country. Progress after that, however, was slower. In 2010, the war in Afghanistan had stretched to become the longest war in U.S. history. Troops remained in Afghanistan until February 2020, when an agreement was signed to remove the U.S. military presence in the country.

Afghanistan was not the only country facing military action in the early 2000s. In March 2003, marines and army troops swept into Iraq at the start of Operation Iraqi Freedom, and the ground war for that country began. U.S. troops were supported by Great Britain, Poland, and Australia. President George W. Bush pushed for the war primarily because intelligence reports claimed that the Iraqis had access to weapons of mass destruction (WMD). It was suggested that these WMD included chemical and biological components that could kill millions. The president was worried that Saddam Hussein would use those weapons on the United States and its allies.

The ground war was violent, but short. In just three weeks, American forces had stormed their way into Baghdad, the capital of Iraq. It seemed the war in that country was drawing to a quick conclusion. However, the Americans never found any evidence that Iraqi forces truly possessed WMD. Years later, the Bush administration admitted its prewar intelligence concerning the WMD was flawed.

Nevertheless, after the fall of Baghdad, a new war began. Supporters of Saddam Hussein and insurgents, who had come from other Middle Eastern countries, fought the Americans. Iraqi ethnic groups fought against each other, and the Americans were often caught in the middle of their battles. Saddam Hussein himself was captured by soldiers on December 13, 2003, but the war raged on regardless. U.S. and allied forces faced fierce resistance, which lasted for years, by fighters from Iraq and other nearby countries. Marines took the lead at First and Second Battles of Fallujah, both in 2004, which were intended to root out the insurgent groups in the city. The second battle proved to be the bloodiest U.S. engagement since the Vietnam War, but the American military was able to clear the city of most of the insurgents.

The war in Iraq officially ended in 2011 when the last U.S. troops were withdrawn from the country. However, part of the al-Qaeda organization in Iraq split and some groups began to reinvade Iraq's western provinces under the name of the Islamic State of Iraq and Syria (ISIS), taking over much of the country and combining the Iraqi insurgency and the neighboring civil war in Syria into one conflict. Presidents Barack Obama and Donald Trump struggled to stamp out the ISIS movement until 2019, when the leader of the group died following a U.S. raid.

A WARTIME HERO: THE LION OF FALLUJAH

Major Douglas Zembiec was a superstar marine recruit. A former high school and college wrestling champion, Zembiec entered USMC training with a leg up on his classmates. He graduated from the U.S. Naval Academy in 1995 and attained the rank of second lieutenant. As the commander of Echo Company in the 1st Marine Division, he led his troops in an attack on the city of Fallujah, Iraq. For his heroics, he earned a Silver Star Medal, a Bronze Star Medal, two Purple Hearts, and an enduring nickname: the Lion of Fallujah.

MORE THAN WAR

Marines have proven time and again that they are ready and willing to be the first to a fight. However, they are also often the first Americans called upon to save lives in global humanitarian efforts. These missions are called "military operations other than war," or MOOTW. During MOOTW, men and women of the Corps are often called upon to deliver food and medicine to civilian communities facing civil strife or natural disasters.

In December 1992, marines landed on beaches in the African nation of Somalia. They were prepared to fight if necessary but hoped to avoid violent conflict. Somalia had been torn by civil war for years. Meanwhile, the people of the nation faced food shortages. The UN and other international agencies sent food, but it was often looted by warring armies. In the 1990s, the marines were deployed as a police force. They protected food supplies and made sure food was properly distributed to hungry people. The soldiers accomplished their mission and hunger was eased in the troubled country. Fittingly, the Somalia MOOTW was called Operation Restore Hope.

Marines are best known as fighters, but their MOOTW actions—such as Operation Restore Hope—are just as heroic.

Marines returned to Africa in June 1997, this time on a rescue mission to the nation of Sierra Leone. A lengthy civil war in the country had left thousands of people killed and wounded. One particularly brutal warring faction took over the country in 1997 and allowed its soldiers to loot stores and attack foreigners. The marines were deployed to take charge of this chaotic situation, working to protect and evacuate foreigners, including a large group of Americans.

In December 2004, a massive tidal wave, called a tsunami, washed over shores in the Pacific. The wall of water killed more than 200,000 people and left millions homeless. Marines joined other international forces to give medical assistance to the injured and help restore order. On the island nation of Sri Lanka, marine bulldozers rolled off naval ships and were immediately used to clear roads of debris and allow emergency supplies to reach cut-off villages. The Corps also conducted airlift missions to help those who had been wounded and displaced.

Closer to home, Hurricane Katrina—the deadliest hurricane since 1928—struck the Gulf Coast in 2005 with a vengeance. Once again, the marines responded. They staged their operations at the Stennis International Airport in Bay St. Louis, Mississippi, and fanned out across the region's flooded areas in amphibious assault vehicles (AAVs) to rescue stranded civilians. Once the water receded, the marines also assisted in cleanup and rebuilding efforts in Mississippi and Louisiana.

In January 2010, a powerful earthquake hit Haiti, causing catastrophic damage to the infrastructure of the island nation and killing more than 200,000 Haitians. In the aftermath, some turned to looting and violence. In response, the marines quickly deployed the 22nd and 24th MEUs to provide security in a place that had become lawless. Amid the disorder, the marines also distributed 1.6 million rations of food, 560,000 liters of water, and 15,000 pounds of medical supplies. Haiti was struck by a powerful earthquake again in August 2021, and the USMC was again ready to provide assistance. This time, more than 200 marines were mobilized in less than 12 hours to arrive off the coast of Haiti.

CHAPTER 4

THE MODERN MARINE CORPS

With around 200,000 members, the USMC is the smallest of the four major military branches (the army, navy, and air force being the other three). With the branch's long history of honorable service, marines are often viewed as the best of the best, ready to spring into action anywhere in the world. They are skilled at conducting amphibious, expeditionary, and air-based missions to protect the interests of the United States and its allies.

MARINES' PLACE IN THE WORLD

Members of the Corps are stationed all across the globe. Marines stand on guard at all U.S. embassies. The islands of Hawaii and Japan have large marine contingents. Of all active marines, most are assigned to the Corps's three infantry divisions, which make up the Fleet Marine Force (FMF). Divisions of the FMF are strategically stationed around the world: the 1st Marine Division is headquartered at Camp Pendleton near Oceanside, California; the 2nd Division is at Camp Lejeune near Jacksonville, North Carolina; the 3rd Division is in Okinawa, Japan.

North Carolina's Camp Lejeune is the home of the 2nd Marine Division, and it often hosts exercises for marines in training.

By and large, marines are still soldiers of the sea. Members of the USMC are highly specialized in amphibious, ship-to-shore warfare. In this capacity, the Corps works closely with the navy.

The Corps also has its own aviation contingent. Marine air units are divided into three units called "wings." Each air wing is attached to an infantry division. Marine pilots fly fighter planes similar to those used by the navy. In combat, the fighter planes provide air support for ground troops. The Corps also maintains a large fleet of helicopters.

MORE THAN A MOTTO

Each branch of the U.S. armed forces has its own motto. Over the years, these mottos have taken a special place in the hearts of soldiers and the American people. Perhaps the most famous military motto is that of the USMC: Semper Fidelis. Often shortened to "Semper Fi," this saying is Latin for "always faithful." Marines take the idea of "Semper Fi" seriously, which means that they are always thinking about how their actions reflect on themselves, the USMC, and their nation. It is also often used as a greeting or send-off among soldiers.

WAITING IN RESERVE

There are more than 35,000 soldiers serving in the Marine Reserves. These servicemen and women are divided into three groups: the Ready Reserve, the Standby Reserve, and the Retired Reserve. Members of the Ready Reserve are required to train for one weekend per month and put in two weeks of full-time duty each year. Ready Reservists are the first to be called into active duty if the need arises. The Standby Reserve is made up of marines who have already served on active duty. Standby soldiers do not have weekend training obligations, but they may also be called up to duty in times of emergencies. Retired Reserves are those who have served 20 years or more in the Corps and are now collecting from their retirement plans, called pensions. Though the likelihood is low, even members of the Retired Reserve can be pressed into emergency duty.

Ready Reservists are sometimes referred to as "part-time marines," based on the reduced amount of training required. This name, however, fails to capture the true fighting spirit within each of the reservists. All members of the Ready Reserve know they can be called up with just a few days' notice and find themselves on active duty overseas shortly after. They are always prepared to honorably serve if necessary.

An example of a typical USMC reserve unit is helicopter squadron HMLA-773, nicknamed the "Red Dogs." This unit, based in New Jersey, comprises soldiers who are established in their civilian careers. The squadron, originally established in 1958, is made up of a few hundred marines and several helicopters. HMLA-773 was activated from the reserves in 2003 and sent to Afghanistan as part of the response to the September 11 attacks.

Members of the Ready Reserve undergo much of the same training as career marines, making them similarly qualified for deployment anywhere in the world.

The Red Dogs served in Afghanistan for a period of six months. While supporting ground troops, they piloted helicopters through snowstorms and through thick fog. Several times, helicopters from the Red Dog squadron engaged in firefights with Afghan rebels on the ground. The marines from HMLA-773 are just a few examples of reservists who have been called up to active duty and served with distinction.

THE HIGHEST RANK

As in all military branches, excellence in the marines comes from leadership. The highest-ranking officer in the USMC is a four-star general, who is called the commandant of the Marine Corps. Those who have served as commandant are among the nation's most decorated soldiers. The commandant is appointed by the president of the United States on the basis of four-year terms. The first commandant was Samuel Nicholas, who served from 1775 to 1783.

A number of famous commandants have risen to legendary status for current and aspiring marines. Archibald Henderson, the fifth commandant, served from 1820 to 1859. No other commandant served in the position for longer than Henderson. For that reason, Henderson is called "the grand old man of the Marine Corps." John Archer Lejeune, the 13th commandant, was in command of the Corps from 1920 to 1929. Lejeune fought in World War I as a marine and later developed the amphibious warfare strategy that the Corps used in World War II. North Carolina's huge Camp Lejeune base is named for this memorable commandant. The 18th commandant, Alexander Archer "Archie" Vandegrift, was the top marine from 1944 to 1947. Early in World War II, Vandegrift commanded the 1st Marine Division during the assault of Guadalcanal. For his iron defense of that island in the face of repeated enemy attacks, Vandegrift was awarded the Medal of Honor.

PLAYING ALONG

Not all who call the Corps home are fighters on the front lines. The Marine Band, for instance, is stationed permanently in Washington, D.C. Consisting of more than 150 musicians, it is the oldest professional band in the United States. The Marine Band is often called "the President's Own" because it performs at all ceremonies and occasions hosted by the president. The band, founded in 1798, traces its history back to the John Adams administration.

Those who are selected to join the Marine Band are enlisted marines, but their path to the Corps is unusual. Band personnel do not receive rifle training and they are not sent to marine boot camp. Members of the Marine Band are generally music majors selected from the nation's best colleges. Many hold advanced degrees in their specialties. The band plays with spirit and technical precision, and the President's Own ranks among the greatest military bands in the world.

Noted composer and bandleader John Philip Sousa presided over the Marine Band from 1880 to 1892. Sousa grew up in Washington, D.C., and loved band music. Under his leadership, the Marine Band marched its way to world fame. Sometimes called the "March King," Sousa composed some of the most inspiring marches ever written, including "Semper Fidelis," "The Washington Post," "El Capitan," and "The Stars and Stripes Forever." Sousa's music is still performed and loved all over the world.

Built in 1806, the historic Marine Barracks is the official home of the Marine Band and the oldest active marine post. Because of its location on the corner of 8th and I Streets in Washington, the Barracks is nicknamed "8th and I." The building also houses the Marine Drum and Bugle Corps, which is often called the "Commandant's Own." A popular show for tourists and Washingtonians alike is the Evening Parade, a lengthy performance that can been seen on Friday evenings during the summer months. The parade features the Marine Band, the Marine Drum and Bugle Corps, and the Marine Corps Silent Drill Platoon.

Just as fighting marines are among the best soldiers in the world, members of the Marine Band are among the best musicians in the world.

CHAPTER 5

BECOMING A MARINE

To maintain its reputation as the nation's legendary fighting force, the USMC sets high standards for new recruits. Young aspiring marines should try to be high achievers in both physical and mental tests. High scores on standardized tests are just as important as the ability to do push-ups. Anyone who wants to join the Corps must also meet general eligibility criteria, including age (only those 18 to 28 may enlist), criminal history (no one convicted of a major crime may enlist), and substance abuse (no one who fails a drug test may enlist).

SO YOU WANT TO BE A MARINE?

The Corps has earned global respect by selecting only the finest recruits. It is best to think of the USMC as an exclusive club. The marines set a high bar for new club members to join. Many young applicants are rejected for a variety of reasons. Some are turned down because they scored low on standardized tests. Some fail to qualify for not meeting physical fitness standards. Still others are turned down because of tattoos or piercings. Despite the qualification standards, the marines have little difficulty filling their ranks with fresh recruits. Many young people interested in the military want to join what they consider to be the best branch.

Meeting general enlistment requirements is the easy part. Those who are accepted into the Marine Corps must also be ready for the tough three-month training program called boot camp.

The aim of boot camp is to reduce recruits' individuality and make them part of a unit. In addition to constant physical and mental training, recruits do not even use pronouns like "I" or "me," because those words reflect individuality. Marines in training often refer to themselves only as "the recruit." To further emphasize that the individual is less important than the unit, male recruits have their heads shaved down to the scalp. This buzz cut makes the young men look generally alike as they train together. Females are allowed to keep their hair, but it must be cut close and kept neat.

The Marine Corps maintains two boot camps, formally called Marine Corps Recruit Depots (MCRDs). One MCRD is in San Diego, California, and male recruits who enlist from areas west of the Mississippi River are trained there. The other MCRD is in Parris Island, South Carolina, and it receives male recruits from locations east of the Mississippi. For many years, all female recruits were trained at Parris Island regardless of their home state. In 2021, however, a new Congressional policy ordered full integration of male and female recruits in San Diego, and the first 53 female recruits graduated from boot camp at that location. Male and female recruits undergo very similar training, but men and women are housed in separate barracks and work in separate units.

The training routine at the two camps is identical, but Parris Island graduates often claim their experience is more challenging because they have to deal with the heat and the biting sand fleas in South Carolina. These marines call their San Diego counterparts "Hollywood Marines" as a jab at the base's California location. It is impossible to determine which is the tougher boot camp, but that has not prevented decades-long arguments between graduates from both MCRDs.

BOOT CAMP

The origin of the "boot camp" name is another legend of the Corps. One story says that, in the old days, the first item issued to a recruit was a pair

In 2021, the first group of female marines graduated from the MCRD in San Diego.

of boots. Another claims that the leggings worn by sailors during the Spanish-American War were called "boots," which became a term for any sailor or marine recruit in the early 1900s. Whatever the origin of the name, boot camp has come to refer to any basic training facility. All branches of the U.S. armed service require basic training for new enlistees, but no other basic training program is tougher than marine boot camp.

Life for a recruit centers around their platoon, which is made up of 80 members. Each platoon is run by four sergeants called drill instructors (DIs). The DI is a demanding boss, a parent figure, and a teacher all at once. Under the watchful eyes of the DI, recruits learn to march with the standard-issue M16 rifle. Recruits also disassemble their rifles, thoroughly clean them, and memorize the proper names of each tiny part. In a few weeks, a recruit should be able to take the rifle apart and put it back together again—blindfolded.

The DI is also a physical education instructor, leading the platoon in lengthy and vigorous exercise sessions. Not everyone can keep up with the challenging program. A small number of recruits, both male and female, are dismissed from the Corps during the three months of boot camp. Some simply cannot meet the daily physical demands of the training; others find that they are not mentally tough enough and are released from boot camp.

About midway through boot camp, recruits receive hands-on weapons training. Recruits start

DIs have a reputation for being aggressive and yelling at recruits constantly. Their harsh attitudes are meant to make trainees stronger.

by practicing various firing positions without actually pulling the trigger. Target shooting is next. Young marines are given points and grades for the accuracy they achieve.

The ultimate physical challenge facing recruits comes in the final week with an ordeal called the Crucible. Over the course of 54 hours, recruits endure a constant stream of physical obstacles and close combat exercises. All these training duties require close cooperation between platoon members. In one cooperation drill, recruits deliberately fall backward into the waiting arms of their fellow trainees. Recruits get only four to eight hours of sleep and are fed limited rations. The Crucible is capped off with a brisk 9-mile (14 km) hike, with each recruit carrying a rifle and full pack.

Two rewards await at the Crucible's conclusion. First, the recruit is served a well-earned hearty breakfast; second, the recruit receives the official Marine Corps emblem—the globe and anchor—to wear on their collar. The emblem is a badge of honor and a symbol of the training they have just endured on the path toward becoming a marine.

Graduation from boot camp is marked with a full dress parade. Each graduate has paid in sweat, pain, and perhaps a few tears to take their place on this parade ground. As a band plays "The Marines' Hymn," the boot camp survivors know they are marines and they will be for the rest of their lives.

LEARNING THE LINGO

Marines in boot camp learn a kind of secret language as they learn to fight. Some terms in this language are shared between the USMC and other branches, but others are uniquely marine in their usage. Below are some common words and phrases used by marines and what they mean:

- The blood stripe: The strip of red fabric found on the sides of marine dress uniform pants
- The few, the proud: An expression of the elite nature of the USMC
- First to fight: An expression reflecting the history of marines being ready to rapidly deploy
- Leatherneck: An alternative name for a marine
- Ooh rah (oorah): A battle cry or sign of enthusiasm

A CUT ABOVE

Young people who sign on for USMC officer training come from the nation's colleges and universities. Some future lieutenants are graduates of the U.S. Naval Academy at Annapolis, Maryland. Other officers-to-be are selected directly from the Corps's enlisted ranks.

Officers make up a smaller percentage of over-all marine personnel than in other armed service branches. In the Corps, senior enlisted soldiers called noncommissioned officers (NCOs) assume a greater leadership role.

Officers do not go to boot camp. Instead, they attend Officer Candidates School (OCS) in Quantico, Virginia. In many ways, OCS is just as physically demanding as boot camp. The future officers learn how to march and fire weapons. The motto of OCS is Ductus Exemplo (Leadership by Example). In other

The USMC base in Quantico houses the OCS, where young future leaders undergo their first round of military training.

words, the junior officers must be ready and willing to do all the tasks and take all the risks expected of enlisted soldiers. Soon after graduation, officers will be leading a platoon in the field. They may even be in a combat situation shortly after their OCS experience. They are expected to set a strong example to command the respect of the enlisted ranks.

Officer candidates face a tough 10-week course. Marines in OCS, just like those in boot camp, are training their bodies as well as their minds. They march and shoot, read and learn, and become all-around leaders. Instead of the Crucible faced by other recruits, however, future officers endue a "War Week," which is a five-day program simulating combat conditions. At the conclusion of OCS, the soldiers are sent to the Basic School, where they are provided six more months of intensive physical training. The most important lesson any young officer learns during this training is that a leader in the USMC must be prepared to be entrusted with the lives of their fellow marines.

CHAPTER 6

FURTHER TRAINING

Recruits must be mentally and physically tough to graduate from boot camp. However, receiving their globe and anchor pin does not mark the end of their training. The next step for fresh marines is actually further schooling. The education they are about to receive will make them model soldiers, shooters, and specialists before they are finally deployed to active duty.

AFTER BOOT CAMP

After successfully completing boot camp, young marines are sent to the School of Infantry. This is a nearly two-month course of intense combat training. During the first two weeks, soldiers learn what is called a Common Skills Package. In this program, marines are trained in detecting and firing at targets in the field. Field shooting like this is a new concept, more advanced than target shooting on the rifle range in boot camp. The School of Infantry also teaches marines how to handle deadly tasks, such as hand grenade throwing and disarming land mines.

Recruits in boot camp learn how to shoot at targets. Marines at the School of Infantry learn how to handle real combat situations.

After completing the Combat Skills course, male marines have traditionally branched off for infantry weapon training. They learn how to effectively shoot with and maintain machine guns, mortars, and antitank missiles. Female marines also learn the Combat Skills Package, but until 2015, they were not trained in special infantry weapons. Formerly, women were not posted on fighting fronts during combat, so they did not need this training. In late 2015, however, new U.S. policy was to allow women on the front lines.

Most marines, once they have graduated from the School of Infantry courses, will be assigned to one of the three infantry divisions. There, they will need no reminder that a marine's primary job is to carry a rifle into battle. The infantry divisions constantly train so they will be ready for combat assignments.

THE IMPORTANCE OF A RIFLE

For more than three decades, marines entered combat with the M16 rifle. Different versions, featuring upgrades and improvements, have been employed over the years, but the base M16 rifle remained the backbone of the Corps for many years. In the late 2010s, however, the Corps began investigating potential replacement rifles for standard infantry, eventually selecting the M27 as the M16's replacement. Though the M27 is heavier than the M16, marines love the new rifle because it is highly accurate and reliable in real combat conditions.

Though the previous standard-issue M16 rifle was well liked, early impressions of the M27 indicate that it is a good replacement.

Marine sniper teams are made up of specialists responsible for covering long-range targets during ground combat missions. In 2002, the marines added a designated marksman to sniper teams, hoping to increase their effectiveness when covering mid- and short-range targets. These designated marksmen use a special semiautomatic rifle—meaning that one bullet is fired with each pull of the trigger—that is designed with accuracy in mind.

NOT-SO-SMALL ARMS

Infantry fighters benefit from the deployment of strong supporting weapons such as artillery, tanks, and armored personnel carriers. The Fleet Marine Force make use of amphibious craft to get the infantry from ships to shores. All of these unique vehicles and weapons require their own specialists to keep them in operation.

Artillery is a special class of weapon, and pieces can propel high explosive shells long distances into enemy-held areas. Most artillery pieces are so big they must be towed behind a vehicle and they are operated by teams, not a single shooter. The core of marine artillery is the 155 mm M777 Howitzer. The M777 has been through several different versions over the years, each one improving accuracy, weight, or usability. A well-drilled marine artillery squad moves with precision as soldiers pass new rounds forward, make an aiming correction, and fire. Experienced M777 crews can fire as many as four shells a minute.

Today, marines are still well known for ship-to-shore assaults. During World War II and the Korean War, amphibious fighting meant taking slow-moving, lightly armored amtracs into battle. Today's seagoing assault vehicles are an incredible improvement. Modern AAVs have armor plating, and they can carry more than 20 combat-ready marines. On land, AAVs travel at 20 to 30 miles (32 to 48 km) per hour; in water, AAVs can move at about 6 miles (10 km) an hour. Another amphibious advancement is the Landing Craft Air Cushion (LCAC) vehicle. Riding on a cushion of air—formed by huge propellers—the LCAC can carry a 600-ton (544 mt) payload over the waves at the astonishing speed of almost 50 miles (80 km) per hour. The air cushion also allows the LCAC to land on a beach and give the marines on board a dry place to disembark.

It is the marines' job to land on hostile shores; it is the navy's job to get them there. The navy uses special amphibious assault ships to transport marines to their assigned locations. The USS *Tarawa* and the USS *Wasp* are examples of assault ships used to transport marines. The vessels look like aircraft carriers almost three football fields in length. Helicopters and light fighter planes can take off from their flat decks. Marines live below decks until they are ordered to board helicopters and landing craft for an assault. The landing craft are housed in the "well decks" of the amphibious ships, which are then flooded to allow the landing craft to exit the ship and travel across the ocean. These ships allow marines to approach enemy shores through the air or over the waves.

The USMC is considered a light infantry force, but it uses the nation's heaviest tank. Fully loaded, the M1A1 Main Battle Tank (used by the army as well as the Marine Corps) weighs in at 67.7 tons (61.4 mt). It is armed with a powerful 120 mm gun that is aimed with the aid of electronic devices. Enhanced targeting techniques allow it to hit a target more than 2.5 miles (4 km) away. The M1A1 is typically crewed by four: a driver, a gunner, a loader, and a commander. It is regarded as the best tank in the world.

The USMC sends its soldiers to battle with top-of-the-line weaponry, including the world-renowned M1A1 tank.

The primary light armored vehicle for the marines is the Light Armored Vehicle-25 (LAV-25). Sometimes called a "battle taxi," the LAV-25 is an armored personnel carrier propelled by eight wheels that brings marines to the fighting fronts. It has an operational crew of three and is capable of carrying six troops. Despite its huge weight—12 tons (11 mt)—the LAV-25 can reach 60 miles (97 km) per hour on the ground. It is also an amphibious vehicle that can run at about 6 miles (10 km) per hour on the water. The LAV-25 is armed with a 25 mm chain gun and a 7.62 mm machine gun.

To defeat enemy tanks and armored personnel carriers, the marines employ a powerful weapon called the Javelin. Small and light enough to be mounted on a marine's shoulder, the Javelin can fire a missile at enemy vehicles more than a mile away. A soldier simply has to load the weapon, sight in on the enemy, and fire. A highly advanced infrared system then guides the missile toward its target.

HEAVIER WEAPONRY

Instead of the standard M27 rifle, some marines deploy to battlefields with the squad automatic weapon (SAW). This machine gun offers greater firepower—and greater weight—than the M27, making it a good option for aggressive combat situations. Though heavier than a regular rifle, a SAW can still be carried by a single soldier and loaded with up to 200 rounds at a time. The USMC has been issuing SAWs since before World War II, including the famously effective Browning Automatic Rifle (or BAR).

THE BEST OF THE BEST OF THE BEST

There are many who believe the United States has the most powerful military in the world. Among its armed service branches, it is often believed that the USMC includes the most elite fighters. The fittest, smartest, and most capable marines are selected to join the United States Marine Corps Force Reconnaissance, making these soldiers the best of the best of the best. Force Recon is responsible for undertaking the toughest advance missions, often behind enemy lines. Members of this unit have to take brutal, extensive training courses so they are ready to parachute into battle, go on lengthy underwater dives, and travel across difficult terrain on foot.

FROM THE SKIES

In addition to amphibious and land-based warfare, the Corps has a mighty presence in the air. Marine aircraft are divided into three categories: fixed-wing, rotary-wing, and—the newest model—tilt-rotor. All three types operate from ships or from land.

Fixed-wing planes include swift fighters and dive bombers. One longstanding marine fighter plane is the F/A-18 Hornet. This twin-jet aircraft can clear enemy planes from the skies while providing ground support for marine infantry. The Hornet is capable of reaching speeds up to 1,100 miles (1,770 km) per hour. The plane has a 20 mm cannon mounted in its nose, and it can carry more than 10,000 pounds

(4,500 kg) of bombs or missiles. Hornets can be launched from aircraft carriers or from advanced land bases.

Another fixed-wing aircraft used by the Corps is the AV-8B Harrier II. The Harrier is slow by military jet standards (its maximum speed is about 660 miles [1,060 km] per hour), but its takeoff is unique. The plane is capable of directing its exhaust downward, providing enough power for the Harrier to take off vertically, much like a helicopter. Vertical launch capabilities reduce the amount of space required for takeoff and landing, making the Harrier very useful in amphibious marine operations. The Harrier can also hover in the air, fly backward, and fly in a very tight circle.

The Corps employs two primary types of helicopters: attack, which are designed to fire on ground targets, and transport, which are designed to move troops or cargo. Helicopters are called rotary-wing aircraft because their propellers rotate to provide lift.

Marine attack helicopters are basically gunships. Attack helicopters fire on enemy ground troops with machine guns or with rockets. The AH-1W Super Cobra has been the helicopter of choice for the USMC since the 1980s. This helicopter carries a 20 mm cannon, rockets, precision-guided missiles, and a crew of two officers. Some missiles mounted on Cobras are designed to shoot down enemy helicopters. The Cobra is capable of reaching speeds of 160 miles (260 km) per hour.

Transport helicopters rapidly mobilize to transport troops on various missions. Though not designed for heavy combat, most transport helicopters are armed with an auxiliary machine gun. One important marine transport helicopter is the CH-46E Sea Knight. The Sea Knight has a crew of four and can carry more than a dozen combat-ready marines. It can travel at 160 miles (260 km) per hour, and it often uses that speed to evacuate wounded marines. In such cases, it becomes a first aid station in the sky. When doing medical evacuation work, the Sea Knight can carry up to 15 stretcher cases and 2 attendants.

For moving cargo, the true marine workhorse is the CH-53E Super Stallion. This mighty rotary-wing aircraft has a crew of four. Almost 70,000 pounds (32,000 kg) of equipment or cargo can be stuffed into the Super Stallion's huge interior.

An old favorite among marine pilots is the UH-1N Huey helicopter. A versatile craft, the Huey can be modified to suit various missions. Different versions of the Huey have served the marines since the 1960s.

The MV-22 Osprey is among the finest troop movers in the world. It is a tilt-rotor plane, which means it combines features of fixed-wing and rotary-wing designs. The Osprey has two rotors mounted on a wing. For takeoffs, the rotors and wing are pointed upward. This allows the craft to rise like a helicopter. In the air, the wings and the rotors are shifted to the level position so the Osprey can fly like a fixed-wing airplane. The rotor and wing shift takes just twelve seconds to complete.

The MV-22 Osprey is just one example of how cutting-edge technology has changed how marines do battle—and how they get there.

The advantages to the Osprey design are many. Carrying two dozen marines, the Osprey lifts straight up, reducing the space necessary for takeoff like a helicopter. In level flight, it flies like an airplane. It is twice as fast and has twice the range of the average helicopter. The Osprey became operational in 2007 and has become a favorite for all kind of missions, including carrying freight, medical transport, and enemy assaults, where it carries loads of marines into and out of combat landing zones.

DRONE SUPPORT

As warfare has evolved over the decades, intelligence—meaning information gathered about an enemy—has become increasingly important. Being able to gather intelligence without putting soldiers' lives on the line is one major advantage of unmanned aerial vehicles (UAVs), more commonly called "drones." The Corps has several operational models of these robotic aircraft, which can serve as eyes in the air. Flying without a pilot, they relay pictures and videos of enemy movements back to ground commanders. Some UAVs are small and look much like model aircraft. Others are much larger and can even be equipped with weapons.

Noncombat drones are just one example of a marine craft not dedicated to operating directly on battlefronts. The Corps also uses trucks and cars for the everyday tasks of hauling food to camps or carting garbage out. These ordinary vehicles are not

The USMC now uses cutting-edge drones for all kinds of missions, from reconnaissance to combat.

as exciting as frontline transports, but they play a vital role in supporting the USMC.

A vehicle seen in all units is the High Mobility Multipurpose Wheeled Vehicle (HMMWV), popularly called the Humvee. A small, rugged truck, the Humvee can easily drive over rough ground where there are no roads. It can be fitted to play a variety of roles. Humvees act as ambulances, antitank missile launchers, and troop carriers all in one. It has served the Corps well for more than three decades. However, the Iraq War exposed a weakness in the Humvee: a lack of armor protection. Marines often patrol in hostile territory aboard Humvees, scouting the enemy. Early patrols in Iraq took terrible casualties when their vehicles rolled over a land mine, got caught by an improvised explosive device (IED), or was hit by a rocket-propelled grenade. Later Humvees arriving in Iraq were equipped with armor protection, which helped save lives.

The most common noncombat vehicle seen in the Corps is the seven ton truck. These trucks transport troops, ammunition, and supplies. They also pull trailers and light artillery guns. These trucks can haul and carry up to 30,000 pounds (14,000 kg) at once. They are not amphibious, meaning they cannot "swim" across water, but a special kit that extends the exhaust pipe and the air intake allows the truck to cross a river up to 7 feet (2 m) deep.

USMC technology has come a long way since the branch was born in the 1700s. Even compared to the weapons and vehicles used in World War I and

World War II, modern military equipment is in a league of its own. Though soldiers are generally associated mainly with fighting, there are many marines who also work on maintaining the Corps's vehicles, making sure they are in good fighting shape in case duty calls.

CHAPTER 7

JOINING THE MARINE COMMUNITY

Marines are an elite group, and members of the Corps often think of their comrades as one big extended family. They work together on the front lines around the world, and they build lasting bonds that do not disappear when they return home. The USMC prides itself on bringing people of diverse racial, ethnic, and economic backgrounds together, making its force stronger, closer, and better.

FIGHTING FOR INCLUSION

For years, the USMC was reluctant to take women into its ranks. The first small unit of women marines served in World War I, and they were employed as clerks. Following World War I, women were again denied entry into the Corps. During World War II, women were once again welcomed in the marines. During World War II, women joined the ranks despite the objections of some older officers and enlisted men.

Nearly 20,000 female marines saw service in World War II. They did not see action on combat fronts during the war, but anyone who thought the Corps was no place for females was handily proven wrong. Some female marines excelled as cryptologists, puzzling out the enemy's coded messages. Some served as typists and stenographers. Still others worked as truck mechanics, providing important support to men on the fighting fronts.

Today, women make up a bit more than 8 percent of the total marine force. Though this number is still inching upward, the Corps is still more male than any other branch of the U.S. armed forces. The average amount of female representation across the marines, army, navy, and air force is closer to 17 percent. With the new 2015 policy allowing female marines to fight on the front lines, it is expected that this number will continue to increase.

Though women have not always had equal opportunities, female marines have always served with distinction.

MARGARET A. BREWER: TRAILBLAZER

Female soldiers and the USMC have not always gotten along, but Brigadier General Margaret A. Brewer helped pave the way for future female fighters when she became the first female marine general in 1978. Though she did not see combat on the front lines, her high rank has made her an idol for young women who aspire to serve in the armed forces. Since the time of her promotion, other female officers have risen high in the USMC, including Carol Mutter, who in 1996 became the highest ranking female marine ever when she became a lieutenant general.

Brigadier General Brewer broke new ground for women who wanted to serve in the USMC.

79

MARINES OF COLOR

The late 1700s, when the USMC was founded, were far different from today. One obvious difference is the way many American fighters viewed racial minorities in the colonies. Throughout its early history, membership in the marines was restricted to whites only. Latinos and Native Americans were only allowed to join just before World War II. Black Americans were admitted into the Corps in 1942, but they were put in segregated units. In 1948, President Harry Truman broke new ground when he signed an order ending policies of segregation in all branches of the armed forces. Still, the marines were slow to integrate their ranks, not achieving full cooperation between different races and ethnic groups until the 1950s.

In the segregated Marine Corps of World War II, a legendary marine named Gilbert H. Johnson rose to heroic status. Johnson had formerly served in the army, and when he came to the Marine Corps in 1942, he was promoted to the rank of field sergeant major and was put in charge of all Black drill instructors. Johnson made certain that every Black soldier in the Corps had access to the best basic training the services could provide.

After USMC units were integrated following World War II, marines of color had more opportunities to succeed. Frank E. Petersen entered the Corps in October 1952 and became one of a handful of Black pilots. Petersen flew combat missions in the

The USMC took full advantage of Black Americans during World War II, though units were segregated based on race.

Korean War and in Vietnam, and in 1979, he became the first Black marine to achieve the rank of general.

Marine Lieutenant Billy Mills, a Native American from the Sioux tribe, is another outstanding marine officer of color. He was also an outstanding long-distance runner. In 1964, he participated in the Olympic Games in Tokyo, Japan, competing in the 10,000 meter run. Before the event, no one believed the marine lieutenant had a chance to win. Americans at the time were simply not competitive at distance events; the 10,000 meter race had never been won by an American athlete. Sioux pride and marine pride motivated Lieutenant Billy Mills. He shocked the experts by winning the race and bringing home the Olympic gold medal.

TAKING CARE OF MARINE HEALTH

In war, it is inevitable that soldiers become wounded and need medical care. However, there are no medics within the USMC itself. As elite fighters, marines are never expected to spend time directly tending to injuries. Instead, the USMC calls on the navy to provide combat medics, called corpsmen, to help marine units. Though corpsmen are not officially members of the USMC, the services they provide make them favorites among marines, who rely on their medical care in the field.

Billy Mills, like most marines, brought honor to the USMC even when he was not fighting.

CONTINUING EDUCATION

A marine is never finished learning. Boot camp can be thought of as grade school. The two-month School of Infantry is the marine equivalent of high school. Beyond that, marines are likely to be assigned to one of dozens of schools that teach specialized skills—not that different from a college. Even men and women who have been in the Corps for more than 15 years can look forward to being reschooled at some point. The life of a marine is one defined by study and change.

The basic MEU is a self-contained force. A typical MEU has anywhere from 1,500 to 3,000 soldiers. These men and women are always prepared to board transports and rush to any troubled spot in the world on short notice. MEUs have their own air elements, their own artillery, and their own vehicles. Each unit requires the services of radio operators, mechanics, and cooks in addition to ground-pounding infantry. Special skills require special training. The marine's job is to learn what they are best at so they can help their team.

In addition to formal education, many marines find their NCOs to be valuable teaching resources. The Corps relies on its NCOs for leadership. An NCO is an enlisted leader and holds a status just below that of a commissioned officer (CO). All men and women ranked corporal and above are considered NCOs, and their leadership skills shine when they can train younger soldiers.

Some of the most dependable NCOs are gunnery sergeants, a rank unique to the Corps. Men and women of this rank are typically the highest-ranked enlisted marines in a platoon. They often take on the role of a tough-as-nails teacher, as they are responsible not just for keeping everyone sharp but leading them in battle as well. They have a lot to offer any young soldier who wants to improve themselves physically or mentally.

CHAPTER 8

A TOUGH, FULFILLING JOB

The USMC is considered among the most challenging armed service units for recruits, but those who graduate from boot camp carry with them a pride that lasts a lifetime. Marines are asked to travel the world, be the tip of the spear during enemy engagements, and gut it out in difficult situations. Those who honorably serve in these duties, however, view their job as a privilege—they are the first line of defense for the United States and its allies.

PRIDE AND PAYMENT

As in all armed service branches, marines take a lot of pride in their work. That work not only provides them a sense of purpose but also a stable income and a full slate of benefits for their families. During boot camp, few young marines have time to think about pay. However, as full-fledged marines, everyone is guaranteed food, housing, and complete health benefits. As long as duties are performed, there is no threat of being laid off. In times of an uncertain

It is not easy to make it as a marine, but the USMC is always in need of talented young recruits.

economy and a poor job market, military service is an appealing option for many young people. However, though it is enough to support a healthy lifestyle, income for recruits is far from luxurious; a private entering boot camp has a military pay grade of E-1, which is about $1,700 per month.

Soldiers who manage their duties professionally and consistently have a chance to climb the ranks, and with greater responsibility comes greater pay. Pay grades in the "E" class (for "enlisted") extend all the way up to the rank of sergeant major, a senior NCO at grade E-9. Commissioned officer grades start at the rank of second lieutenant (O-1) and reach as far up as five star general (O-10). Though very few soldiers are promoted to these heights, any marine can make a great living and support their family with enough dedication and a strong work ethic.

Few former soldiers want to talk about pay, but retired marines carry a pride that lasts long beyond one's discharge. The marine experience is something a person will talk about, think about, and remember for a lifetime. In fact, many veterans believe that a person never stops being a marine—once they have graduated boot camp, they are part of the USMC family for life.

CORPS CAREER PATHS

Most marines start by serving a three- or four-year obligation, or commitment, in the Corps and then return to civilian life. They will find that their marine training is an invaluable experience in the years ahead. Infantry training, which all marines go through, teaches a person discipline and a sense of responsibility. Special skills, such as mechanical repair or truck driving, can apply directly to civilian jobs.

After serving their initial commitment, some men and women will decide to remain in the Corps instead of returning to civilian life. For most, the goal is to establish a career and serve the marines for 20 or more years before retiring. After 20 years of service, marines receive a generous pension.

As the initial enlistment period expires, the Corps encourages its men and women to "ship over," or reenlist. It benefits the Marine Corps to keep experienced men and women in its ranks, and when one ships over, they receive a cash bonus. Reenlisting marines generally sign up for three or six additional years. Often, upon shipping over, a marine will get their choice of assignments, giving them greater flexibility in their day-to-day jobs.

Many interesting jobs and assignments are available to career marines. More than 180 specialized skills are taught in marine schools. Soldiers can learn about electronics, weather forecasting, office management, construction, and dozens of other trades. But never forget, marines are fighters first and foremost. At any time during the course of a career, one can expect a transfer to a combat unit.

FAMOUS FORMER MARINES

Most marines live out a successful career in the Corps and then return to a normal civilian life. Some soldiers, however, go on to achieve worldwide recognition for their achievements beyond the battlefield. Below are some of the most successful former marines in history:

- Adam Driver (actor)
- Bob Mathias (Olympic champion and congressman)
- Bum Phillips (National Football League coach)
- Drew Carey (comedian and actor)
- Glen Bell (founder of Taco Bell)
- James Mattis (former U.S. Secretary of Defense)
- John Philip Sousa (composer and musician)
- Jon Corzine (former governor and senator)
- Oliver North (politician and author)
- Rob Riggle (comedian and actor)

Marines are capable of leaving the service to achieve success in a variety of fields, as comedian and actor Rob Riggle did after exiting in 2013.

REWARDS FOR HONORABLE SERVICE

When there is an occasion for marines to wear dress uniforms, they have an opportunity to show off the medals they have received for bravery, heroism, and overall excellent service. Below is a list of some awards that can be given to marines, listed in order of precedence:

- Medal of Honor: The highest award given by the U.S. military; awarded for personal acts of valor above and beyond the call of duty.
- Navy Cross: Awarded to navy personnel and marines for exceptional heroism in combat.
- Navy Distinguished Service Medal: Awarded to officers who perform their duties with excellence.
- Silver Star: Awarded for bravery beyond one's duty.
- Bronze Star: Awarded for exceptional performance in military operations.
- Purple Heart: Awarded to those wounded or killed in combat.

THE ONE SHARED JOB

Fighting in conflicts is the one job shared by everyone in the Corps. All marines are prepared for war, even though they hope they will never be called upon to fight. War is the most brutal, the most hurtful, the most dangerous activity engaged in by humankind, and it has touched the lives of many marines. Traditionally, marines are given tough and dangerous combat assignments. In the early 21st century wars in Iraq and Afghanistan, there were no routine patrols or easy assignments. Wounds suffered during combat range from temporary hearing loss to life-changing injuries. Because IEDs were commonly used in these Middle Eastern conflicts, many soldiers suffered from destroyed limbs, bad body burns, and traumatic brain injuries. War has only gotten more dangerous over the decades, but thankfully, medical techniques have similarly improved. The survival rate among the wounded is far greater than in any previous war. Most marines who suffer combat wounds live to tell the tale, though they may still be scarred, either physically or emotionally.

The stress of battle can be damaging to more than just a soldier's body. Most minds can endure only so much intense danger, only so many close brushes with death. Even after leaving a combat zone, memories of combat danger can invade a soldier's inner thoughts. Veterans of any war can suffer from what is called post-traumatic stress disorder (PTSD). This condition was called "shell shock" in World War I and "combat fatigue" in World War II, but recent research has revealed much more about the issue. PTSD is a mental disorder caused by the stress of war. Nightmares, an inability to concentrate, irritability, and frightening flashbacks to scenes of combat haunt a victim of PTSD.

There are undoubtedly great benefits to a career with the USMC, but there is also danger. Anyone wishing to join the marines must weigh the risks against the rewards. Though many young people who start their careers with the armed service go on to achieve great things, it must be remembered that the ultimate task for a marine is to wage war.

THE FUTURE AND THE PAST

In the 21st century, war is defined by advanced technology. New weapons, tactics, and equipment are always in development, which means that there is always a need for strong and capable soldiers—many of them marines. It also means that war has evolved from simply standing on a battleground and aiming a gun. The Corps employs soldiers who are experts at driving trucks, operating amphibious vehicles, flying UAVs, and repairing equipment, just as it employs more traditional fighters. A career path in the Marine Corps is a wide open world for any young person who is excited about defending the United States. For more than 200 years, the USMC has built a reputation as one of the world's premier fighting forces, and this tradition of excellence is one thing that never changes, no matter the latest rifle or drone. The Corps is always ready to welcome a recruit who can carry this past into the future, just as marines have done every day since 1775.

GLOSSARY

boot camp Marine basic training (usually a three-month course) given to all marine enlisted men and women.

casualty A soldier wounded or killed in war.

chaotic Extremely confusing.

coalition A group of countries allied in a conflict.

commandant The top-ranked marine, usually a four-star general.

contingent A small military unit.

dismiss To tell to leave.

displaced Forced to move, often by a natural disaster.

elite Superior, better than others.

escalate To increase or grow greater; the term was often used to describe how the Vietnam War expanded year by year.

ethnic group A group of people with similar racial and cultural backgrounds.

fixed-wing aircraft Any airplane with a fixed or standard wing.

mobilize To prepare troops for action.

morale Attitude, especially among people during wartime.

mutiny The act of forcibly taking over a ship.

post-traumatic stress disorder (PTSD) A disorder that may develop after a person is exposed to traumatic events.

reluctant Slow to act or commit.

robotic Operated as, or by, a machine.

ship over To reenlist in the Marine Corps.

symbolize To represent an object with another object, as a flag represents a nation.

tsunami A massive tidal wave.

versatile Flexible, usable in many different ways.

Vietcong Vietnamese resistance fighters who fought Americans in the Vietnam War.

Marine Corps Association
715 Broadway Street
Quantico, VA 22134
(866) 622-1775
Website: mca-marines.org
Facebook: @marinecorpsassociation
Instagram and Twitter: @MCA_Marines
The Marine Corps Association is a membership organization for current and former marines. It offers professional development resources and other information for soldiers.

MarineParents.com
PO Box 1115
Columbia, MO 65205-1115
Website: www.MarineParents.com
Facebook: @MarineParents
This organization provides a selection of resources to help young aspiring marines—and their parents—gain a better understanding of the recruitment, training, and deployment process.

National Museum of the Marine Corps
18900 Jefferson Davis Highway
Triangle, VA 22172
(877) 653-1775
Website: www.usmcmuseum.com
Facebook, Instagram, and Twitter: @USMCMuseum
This official museum preserves and celebrates the long and rich history of the marines. It frequently offers special exhibitions.

United Service Organizations (USO)
2111 Wilson Boulevard, #1200
Arlington, VA 22201
Website: www.uso.org/
Facebook and Instagram: @theUSO
Twitter: @the_USO
The USO is a not-for-profit organization that supports men and women in the armed services and helps them connect with their families back home.

United States Marine Corps
3000 Marine Corps Pentagon
Washington, DC 20350-3000
Website: www.marines.mil
Facebook and Instagram: @marines
Twitter: @USMC
The Marine Corps maintains an online presence that includes all the information a young recruit could need, including background information and requirements for enlisting.

Doyle, David. *US Marine Corps in Vietnam: Vehicles, Weapons, and Equipment.* Atglen, PA: Schiffer Military, 2021.

Garstecki, Julia. *Marine Raiders Regiment.* Mankato, MN: Black Rabbit Books, 2019.

Goldsmith, Connie. *Women in the Military: From Drill Sergeants to Fighter Pilots.* Minneapolis, MN: Twenty-First Century Books, 2019.

Green, Michael. *US Marine Corps in the Second World War: Rare Photographs from Wartime Archives.* Havertown, PA: Pen & Sword Military, 2018.

Greer, Andrew. *Reckless: Pride of the Marines.* Mount Pleasant, SC: Arcadia Press, 2017.

Hamen, Susan E. *Life in the US Marine Corps.* San Diego, CA: BrightPoint Press, 2021.

Institute for Career Research. *Career Opportunities in the United States Marine Corps: Wanted, a Few Good Men ... and Women.* Chicago, IL: Institute for Research, 2006.

Johnson, E. R., and Lloyd S. Jones. *United States Marine Corps Aircraft Since 1913.* Jefferson, NC: McFarland & Company, 2018.

Kelley, C. Brian, and Ingrid Smyer-Kelly. *Proud to Be a Marine: Stories of Strength and Courage from the Few and the Proud*. Naperville, IL: Cumberland House, 2017.

Shoup, Kate. *Life as a Navajo Code Talker in World War II*. New York, NY: Cavendish Square Publishing, 2018.

Westermeyer, Paul W. *The United States Marine Corps: The Expeditionary Force at War*. Havertown, PA: Casemate, 2019.

INDEX

ABOUT THE AUTHOR

Siyavush Saidian is a professional editor living in Rochester, New York. When not reading, writing, and working, he keeps his childlike spirit thriving by spending time with his wife and dogs.

CREDITS

Designer: Michael Flynn; Editor: Siyavush Saidian